Sorry, but this is My Stroke!

Not Yours!

By Shani Shamah – A "Stroke ~~Survivor~~ Champion"

2015

It is "My" stroke because people have the habit of asking how "we" are doing today.

Due to circumstances beyond my control, I apologise for the level of English language and grammar. Or in fact, the illogical order - but it is all despite any cognitive impairment I still have.

All royalties (if there are any) will be donated to the UK Stroke Association, and not put into my retirement slush fund…Please note that the Stroke Association UK had no input into this book and does not endorse the information nor the publication in any way.

Thanks to my hubby, friends and family, and especially to all the Stroke and Rehabilitation teams at Northwick Park Hospital.

Contents

Images reproduced with credit and kind permissions from:

Figure 1	The Stroke Association UK
Figure 4	The Stroke Association UK
Figure 5	The Stroke Association UK
Figure 9	The Stroke Association UK
Figure 10	Mike de Kievith
Figure 26	Mayastoso
Figure 32	The Stroke Association UK
Figure 37	Tony Naylor, Tone Cartoons
Figure 40	Royston Robertson, Roystoncartoons
Figure 43	Royston Robertson, Roystoncartoons
Figure 44	Dave Upton Cartoons
Figure 48	Tony Naylor, Tone Cartoons

Introducing a Stroke

But what is a Stroke?

Strokes are not always as obvious as other illnesses, however the effects are, and can be, just as devastating and long lasting.

A stroke is a "brain attack" and it happens when the blood supply to part or all of the brain is suddenly cut off or reduced. As blood carries essential nutrients and oxygen to the brain, without blood your brain cells can become damaged or even die. Strokes are a medical emergency and prompt treatment is essential because the sooner you receive treatment for a stroke, the less damage is likely to happen.

- **Stoke is a 'brain attack'**
- It is a **sudden** loss of blood flow and oxygen to the brain
- It can be caused by a blockage or a blead. As a result brain cells die
- Even a small area of damage can result in significant disability
- Brain function affects the opposite side of the body so if the damage is on one side, the impact may be on the other

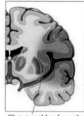

Clot stops blood supply to an area of the brain

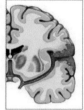

Hemorrhage/blood leaks into brain tissue

Figure 1

Dead brain cells can't start working again, but those just surrounding this area may recover as the swelling caused by the stroke goes down. Also it is possible that other parts of the brain can learn to take over from areas that have died. Be aware a stroke can happen to anyone – fit or otherwise, at any time.

When a stroke happens vital connections within the brain are lost and mobility, speech, eyesight, and concentration, energy and memory can all be damaged.

The brain is responsible for everything we do. The severity of the symptoms depends on how much damage is done to the brain. The main symptoms of a stroke are physical problems in one or both sides of the body (numbness, weakness), drooping in one side of the face, speech problems (slurred speech, muddled words) and visual problems (blurred vision, loss of vision). What part of the brain is affected is usually quite random – **A stroke does not choose sides**. In more serious cases, the person might lose consciousness. The onset-of-stroke symptoms are usually sudden.

Transient ischemic attack (TIA)

A TIA (transient ischemic attack) is often referred to as a mini-stroke or a 'warning stroke'. TIA symptoms are quite similar to a full blown stroke in that it is caused by an interruption in blood flow to the brain, usually from a blood clot. Symptoms also typically last a relatively short-time and could resolve on their own.

Although each person's stroke can be different in general terms, a stroke is a disruption in the blood supply to the brain. Many strokes are caused by blockages (usually blood clots), which disrupt the brain's blood supply. These are called **ischaemic** strokes.

Some strokes are caused by bleeds. These are called **haemorrhagic** stroke

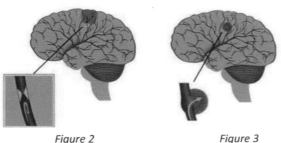

Figure 2   Figure 3

Each person is affected differently by a stroke and individual symptoms depend on which parts of the brain are affected and for what specific functions these parts of the brain are/were responsible. The severity of the symptoms depends on how much damage is done to the brain. The main symptoms of a stroke are physical problems in one or both sides of the body (numbness, weakness, muddled words) and visual problems (blurred vision, loss of vision). The part of the brain that is affected is usually quite random. Most strokes are caused by damaged arteries (the blood vessels through which blood flows from the heart to the rest of the body). Damage to the arteries carrying blood to the brain can cause strokes in the same way that damaged arteries in the heart can cause heart attacks. Our arteries tend to harden, narrow and weaken as we get older but people with high blood pressure, smokers, people with high cholesterol, and people with heart disease or diabetes (or a family history of heart disease or diabetes) are at an increased risk. *Ischaemic strokes* are caused by blockages (usually blood clots) in one of the arteries supplying the brain. Clots can form in these arteries themselves or form in a blood vessel elsewhere in the body and travel to the brain. Clots commonly form where arteries have narrowed due to a build-up of fatty deposits (cholesterol) on their inner walls. The narrowing or furring of the arteries is called atherosclerosis. Although stroke affects the brain and not the heart, people with an irregular heartbeat (atrial fibrillation) are at an increased risk. An irregular heartbeat can cause blood clots which can travel to the brain and cause a stroke. *Haemorrhagic strokes* are caused by one of the blood vessels supplying the brain bursting and causing a bleed. The most common cause is high blood pressure which damages and weakens the arteries making them more likely to tear. Some people have haemorrhagic strokes because they have aneurysms (balloon-like swellings in the arteries) which burst. If an aneurysm bursts and causes bleeding over the surface of the brain, it is called a subarachnoid haemorrhage (SAH). Serious head injuries can also cause haemorrhagic strokes.

The onset-of-stroke symptoms are usually sudden. Strokes can occur while people are sleeping. If this happens, people can wake up with the symptoms. People might also experience longer-term effects such as psychological problems (for example, depression or difficulty controlling emotions), bowel or bladder problems (incontinence) and problems with swallowing. Other symptoms can include pain, dizziness and balance problems, memory problems, a loss of awareness of one side of the body (neglect) and fatigue.

Most strokes are caused by damaged arteries (the blood vessels through which blood flows from the heart to the rest of the body). Damage to the arteries carrying blood to the brain can cause strokes. The brain depends on a supply of blood for the oxygen and nutrients it requires to function properly. When the blood supply is disrupted, brain cells are starved of oxygen and nutrients. This causes damage to the brain tissue. A Stroke is a medical emergency. If you suspect someone is having a stroke, call 999/911 as quickly as possible.

| Facial weakness | Arm weakness | Speech problems | Time to call 999 |

You only need one symptom to indicate a stroke

Figure 4

Strokes can affect people of any age but are more common in older people. Some people have a temporary blockage in the blood supply to their brain which clears of its own accord, quickly and before any lasting damage to the brain is done. This is called a transient ischaemic attack (TIA). Symptoms (rather than cause) also typically last a relatively short time and might resolve on their own.

What are the likely impacts of a stroke?

A stroke can have all sorts of different effects – many are physical that you can see and recognise easily, but there can also be hidden effects, like emotional changes although feelings or thoughts can be seen, changing emotions often lead to a change in behaviour which may signify that all is not well.

This is because a stroke affects the brain, and our brain controls our behaviour and emotions. Injury from a stroke may make a person forgetful, careless, irritable or confused. Stroke survivors may also feel anxiety, anger, depression or frustration. You are likely to experience a rollercoaster of emotions.

Some possible hidden effects:

- Loss of short and/or long term memory
- Depression;
- Changes in vision;
- Personality changes;
- Loss of balance and coordination;
- Changes in sensation;
- Fatigue;
- Loss of relationships and family role;
- Loss of work and financial security

Some possible physical effects of a stroke:

- Weakness
  - Weakness of an arm, leg or both (this is probably the most common and widely recognised effect caused by a stroke.)

- Experiencing problems with movement. (Weakness can vary in its severity. Some people may have very mild weakness in one part of their body, for example their arm, leg or face. But for many people its affects one whole side of their body. This is called hemiparesis.)
- Paralysis. (Differs slightly from weakness as it describes the loss of the ability the term hemiplegia is used to describe paralysis of one whole side of the body.)

Having weak or paralysed muscles can affect your movement. For example, if you have weakness in your leg you may find it difficult to get in or out of bed, to stand or walk. Arm weakness can make it more difficult for you to do daily tasks such as washing and dressing.

- Some people also have problems with balance after a stroke. Spasticity is a condition that can develop if you have weakness or paralysis after your stroke. It is a form of muscle tightness - your muscles become tense and can contract abnormally. I would be sat in front of a full length mirror and told to sit up straight and not lean over to one side or the other – to me I was straight. I never had good posture anyway.
- Muscles need some sort of tightness (called muscle tone) as without this they would be floppy and not able to work. Following a stroke, a muscle may have very low tone when it is weak, for example you may not be able to hold your arm up without support. If muscles recover, it is expected that the tone will increase to normal. However, some weak and damaged muscles develop high tone. The muscle feels stiff and can become painful. This is called spasticity and it can happen when you are resting, or it can affect you when moving the muscle. Use it or lose it!

"People don't always need advice sometimes really all they need is a hand to hold and an ear to listen and a heart to understand them no matter what their circumstances"

Many disabilities resulting from a stroke improve with time. Behaviour changes and emotional health can also improve over time, but everyone is different just as each stroke is different.

As a result of a stroke, connections in the brain, also called **neural pathways**, may be damaged. And this damage may interrupt the normal flow of signals within the brain and between the brain and other parts of the body. Simple everyday tasks can become an uphill struggle, it is a new beginning in getting to know your new body and what it is capable of doing post-stroke.

What drives the brain to re-connect, and what drives other parts of the brain to take over the function, might be influenced by the amount of repetition and the amount of therapy. Many stroke survivors may experience strong progress early on in their physical and occupational therapy programs, but can taper off after an initial burst. It doesn't mean they aren't making progress. They have a slower rate of progress. **You need to be patient and determined** – because if you have the **drive and determination to succeed**, it is amazing what you can achieve, I should know as I have been there, "bought the 't'-shirt and sent the postcard" as they say but please **be patient as progress does take time. Again, just work hard and be patient.**

And because neural repair can take place for years after a stroke, some stroke survivors will continue to see some recovery several years after a stroke. However, there are parts of the brain that once damaged can never re-grow but other parts may be able to repair by doing **repetitive functional tasks.**

However, the most common effects of a stroke are more physical such as weakness and actual loss of use of limbs, such as legs and arms and problems with balance.

The brain controls everything we do, including the way we move. It is divided into 2 hemispheres, left and right. The left hand side of the brain is mainly concerned with language, and movement on the right hand side of the body. Nerve cells (sometimes called neurons) are stimulated by the brain and send electrical messages to our muscles to stimulate them to move. If the brain cells controlling those nerve cells are damaged by a stroke, the messages can't be sent and the muscles can't move.

Too many people have preconceived ideas of what a stroke actually means/is and that included me as I thankfully never knew anybody that actually had suffered a stroke before. I now know differently. The hospital staff kept saying that I knew what the consequences of a stroke were – well actually not, as I have never had one before, it is not like having a cold or the flu. The consequences of a stroke can be quite severe for the body and not only for brain injury but muscle weakness and spasms, such as uncontrollable shaking, as well. **Don't let a stroke control you, take control, and you control it**. Keep your sense of humour and keep positive – wonderful tonics for recovery. What defines us is how well we rise after falling, but be resilient, even though you might feel that you will never smile or laugh again, "shoot for the moon even if you miss you will land among the stars", especially when you are frightened and wondering what the hell is happening to you, even though it can feel that life was/is very unfair you will come out the other side eventually even if it is with an intermittent brain. Learn to cope with strategies – complaining won't change the outcome but a positive attitude will!

Facial	Arm	Speech	Time
weakness	weakness	problems	to call 999

Figure 5

What are the treatments?

For investigating strokes, the key test is a brain scan or you might have a CT (Computerised Tomography) scan or an MRI (Magnetic Resonance Imaging) scan. Your scan results can show whether your stroke is ischaemic (clot) or haemorrhagic (bleed). This is important because the treatments differ significantly depending on the type of stroke. You might also have an ultrasound test to check for any blockages in the main arteries in your neck which supply your brain with blood (the carotid arteries). Your blood pressure will be checked, you will have blood tests to check your cholesterol and glucose levels, and other tests to check your heart.

People who have had a stroke are at an increased risk of further strokes so it is important to try to reduce this risk. If your stroke was ischaemic you might be given medication to thin your blood and so reduce your risk of blood clots. If you have high blood pressure or high cholesterol you might be given medication to reduce and control your levels. A small number of people having ischaemic strokes might benefit from a treatment called thrombolysis which dissolves the clot blocking an artery. This treatment needs to be given within a short period of time after the onset of symptoms (within three hours). It can significantly reduce the effects of the stroke but it is not available in all hospitals and is not suitable for everyone. If you have a partial blockage in your carotid artery you might benefit from surgery to clear it. This operation is called a carotid endarterectomy. Your doctors and/or medical team will discuss your suitability for this procedure with you and your family.

In the Emergency Room

Once a stroke patient has been called in by the ambulance crew, the emergency room personnel immediately begin preparing, they are/should be ready to receive the patient as soon as they hit the door – This should trigger the clock ticking meaning doctors and nurses must work quickly to meet a stringent timeline of tests, including blood tests and a CT scan so that a blood clot busting drug called tissue plasminogen activator (t-PA) can be administered. If necessary and appropriate - Everything must be done in a timely manner as there are much rigid timelines that have to be/should be achieved. This is because t-PA can only be used if the diagnosis is made and t-PA is administered within an hour of arrival, where an obstruction exists in a blood vessel that is supplying blood to the brain. t-PA dissolves the obstruction, allowing blood flow to the brain.

Tests for sugar, cholesterol levels and clotting speed will be taken as well as blood pressure.

Now the hard work begins.

Suddenly Everything Changes – My Personal Story

Who am I and what's my story?

I am not hot nor gorgeous, and I don't have an amazing figure nor a flat stomach. In fact, I am far from being considered a model but I am me. I eat food, I have more fat than I should, and I have scars and I have a history. Some people love me, some like me, some hate me, I have done good, I have done bad, I love my bed socks and my bed rugby shirts, and I go out without makeup. I am random and crazy and don't pretend to be someone I am not. You can love me or not, I won't change and if I love you, I do it with my heart. I make no apologies for the way I am, I come with baggage, but I am me, with my pregnancy stretch marks – bio oil did not work for me. What you see is what you get.

Figure 6

Take me or leave me; accept me or walk away; love me or hate me, but don't make me feel less of a person if I don't fit into your idea of who I should be.

I am me and I love me as I am!

"I know that I am weird. It sometimes makes me laugh, and that makes me super happy!"

I love rumours as I always find out amazing things about myself I never knew.

Figure 7

I am a 56-year-old mother of four and grandmother to 3 little ones. I did not smoke nor drink and did not have a too stressful job in my later life and my blood pressure was always on the low side. Note that it is sometimes said that stress is a result of modern civilization. That in the simpler cultures of the past, one had major decisions taken by a benevolent feudal superior, in short, stress is in large measure a consequence of emancipation, education, greater opportunity and 'progress'. Looking back now, I think I just fell off the treadmill! It feels like you have been knocked over by a juggernaut.

It was Easter Good-Friday 2013 (perhaps not so good for me!). My body obviously had different ideas. I was in the middle of cooking some meals for my mother who had just had a hip replacement operation. I would normally have been stressed as my son was home from university and is the one who would usually have been shouted at, but on this day I had not shouted at him once to tidy his bedroom or bathroom or to make his bed – no joke – you would also be stressed with this mess how on earth he can live like this? I will never know he just lives on a different planet. If you didn't know the boy, then you would think his room had been burgled! – Just not quite tidy yet.

Figure 8

Ground-Zero

I was in the kitchen and suddenly felt as if I was foaming at the mouth and generally not feeling well - so I rushed downstairs to lie down (our bedroom is on the ground floor). My husband recognised the F.A.S.T symptoms and immediately called 999/911.

Facial weakness **Arm** weakness **Speech** problems **Time** to call 999

Figure 9

I told him not to be so silly as I was not having a stroke but as usual he took no notice of me as I am (she who must be obeyed!) And thank goodness he didn't on this occasion. The paramedic arrived first of all and after checking all my basic vital signs, like blood pressure and asking an awful lot of questions, he then requested the ambulance - within 5 minutes the ambulance arrived - luckily both the paramedic and the ambulance were in the area. There is a popular parking spot for emergency vehicles just right for a coffee (or 'smoking') break. Within less than an hour I was having a CT brain scan in hospital. My husband was asked whether we both agreed for me to be administered with a "clot busting" drug which dissolve clots, one of which I had in my brain and we were warned of the risks of doing that. We both agreed immediately as we could really see no alternative. They administered the drug and I was wheeled onto the Hyper Acute Stroke Unit (HASU) – a specialist unit staffed by experts in looking after patients in the first few hours and/or days following a stroke. Here I was closely monitored and specialist tests were carried out to try and find out what sort of stroke had occurred and what damage it had done and why it happened.

My first few hours

Until I accepted the fact that I had had a stroke I was very anxious, nervous and scared and yes, I admit now - depressed - as this experience was all new to me and it was a case of the unknown and everything was moving far too quickly and I just went with the flow. **But don't be afraid to ask what and why** - which I never did - I suppose it is a bit like the time until you acknowledge and stand up and admit you are an alcoholic (which I hasten to add I am not, nor was I), then your recovery will be delayed. It took me quite a while to accept the fact – I was in denial.

My husband watched as my brain functions, shut down one by one. Motion, speech, and self-awareness –as my brain in effect completely deteriorated in its ability to process any information.

Every second counts – especially as the brain is an extremely complex organ that controls various body functions as a stroke does not takes sides – for example if a stroke occurs in the brain's right side then it is more than likely that the left side of the body is affected but not everyone is the same and a stroke can affect people in different ways. You only need one of the F.A.S.T. elements to happen for a potential stroke – **not necessarily all at once.**

Everything moved so fast, I would have liked a minute or so to breathe and take it all in – a "time-out" would have been appreciated.

Figure 10

I had a rapid assessment –by doctors that I later learned was a specialist team at the hospital.

I had monitoring and physiological intervention in a high-dependency bed/ward - a multidisciplinary team was on call 24 hours a day, including consultant neurologists, neurosurgeons, interventional radiologists, specialist nurses and therapists, and assessment to assure that I had a smooth transfer of care to any hospitals or wards that I might have needed later.

I had monitoring and physiological intervention. I was in a high-dependency bed – where I needed to think, to walk, and to talk!

The two strokes damaged the right side of my brain, one a clot and the other a bleed. I lost the ability to use anything on my left side, but in effect this unleashed a torrent of 'creative' activity –of work-rounds from my right side. My right side in effect started to compensate for the loss of use of my left side and really took over and still does to this day.

My first few days

Cognitive and emotional effects, plus decision making and memory problems after the stroke. Everything that was happening was too much for me to compute and take in. I had to adjust to limited brain capacity – everything became a blur – in fact I would say I felt lost. – Nothing I could compare it to. Not exactly a welcome mat on the door step. Even though everyone were more than 'hospitable'.

Suddenly I thought that it is times like this that you realise that you have not shaved your legs in a while!

Plenty of constant questions – like; "what is your name and do you know where you are and what happened to you", the torch shining in your eyes - used especially with head injuries. I was asked about head pain and to make sure I heard the voice – checking verbal response and eye opening to see how orientated you are. I always got the day and date wrong.

I rationalised that my excuse for getting the year wrong was to make myself a year younger than I am – I would always ask who ever came in first what the day was and I still got it wrong – ah well cause for some amusement, if nothing else.

Stroke rehabilitation began and my heart rate and rhythm were monitored continuously via sticky gel dots on the chest – but be warned the gel is cold –blood pressure was measured via a cuff on the upper arm and if it gets a little too tight, it can feel as if your arm is about to explode - but hang in there. Additionally, the level of oxygen in the blood is also measured using a clip on the tip of a finger or toe and oxygen may be given via a face mask or nasal prongs.

The noise these machines make sounds worse than it actually is. It can be a very noisy environment with all the monitors bleeping away but do ask for them to be put on 'night mode' which does reduce the noise a little – not very helpful if you have a headache. The noise the machines made reminded me to think of the noise in terms of Pacman (it was an 80's arcade game where an unstoppable Pacman monster eats its way around a maze). And space-invaders (another 80's arcade game- yes I did have a misspent childhood) which had five rows of alien invaders as shown below with the player-controlling a laser cannon at the bottom of the screen. And directly above the laser cannon there are defence bunkers.

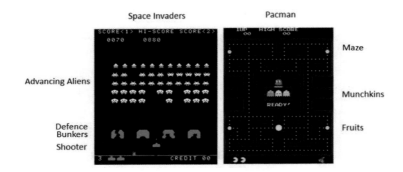

Figure 11

In the very early days I remember one of my daughters visiting me on this ward and asked what had happened to the other patients on the ward. – she has a very similar sense of humour to me – I told her: "Shhhh! Do not to say anything but I think they all had strokes!" – well it does not take a genius to work that one out as I was on the stroke ward after all. Touchy-feely tendencies are well known in the family especially amongst the older members of the family (on my husband's side not mine), but as luck would have it,

26

those genes have been passed down through the generations as one of my other daughters got thrown off the ward as apparently, the sign "stroke patients here" meant something completely different to her!

The unit then continued my treatment and assessment to see if they could determine the cause of the stroke and its effects. Be warned some results take longer than others to confirm.

My first thoughts

"Oh fruit gums, oh sugar (actually not quite in those terms but close enough to oh f.) – I don't want to become a burden to my family and will I have to go into a care home? – Remember your kids choose your care home for you in later years anyway – so be nice to them from an early stage. Thoughts/questions that went through my mind were why me? – What had I done? For this to have happened- I always thought I led a healthy life – but obviously I was wrong – maybe I should have drunk and smoked then at least I would have known what to change."

At some stage I knew I was on my way out but decided that I was not about to give up without a fight – I was not ready for the scrapheap yet. I am very nosey, and I wanted to see which one of my "girlfriends" would make a beeline for my hubby – well girls if you want a piece of my left overs, certainly not crumbs/castoff with all the commitments and dirty laundry that comes with him (including an awesome mother-in-law. Old-lady! Or Mrs P as she is known) You are going to have to wait quite some time as I am not finished with him yet! There ain't no six-pack on this guy, he is not fat it is just puppy fat. We are going to grow old and wrinkly together.

However if you can get him to loose some wight, then he is all yours – enjoy!

Figure 12

My first few weeks

Really important tip: Delegate one member of the family to be the spoke person for fielding all enquiries etc. and use today's technology for passing the updates around. Use something like Facebook friends.

If after a stroke you can't swallow properly there is a risk that food and drink may get into your lungs- if you do have difficulty then you may be given pureed food or thickened drinks, also you could have fluids through a drip to stop you getting dehydrated and receive your medication in a safe way. Your overall recovery will be better if you can start to eat and drink again through a tube – I had a tube fitted which was removed at some point after a number of weeks – in fact it came out on its own accord – honest it wasn't me who took it out it was in fact a nasogastric tube, which went up my nose and down my throat into the stomach – there is also a gastrostomy tube which goes straight into the stomach I was still able to brush my teeth regularly and I was given wet mouth swabs to help keep my mouth moist – that was horrible if the truth be known.

Quite a lot of the first few days/ weeks in hospital were a blur and I even now have some flashbacks – like I seem to remember that when I was first taken into A&E my feet were cold and I wanted to put on a pair of socks –quite an achievement because it has taken me over 2 years to be able to do this simple task properly again and I seem to remember the consultant asking if I wanted a hand and I replied in my usual fashion and said no thanks and clapped my hands – oh yes quite the joker!! - I was amused by that one. I am not sure the team treating me at the time appreciated my comment as I was then asked to count down from 100 by 7 each time– having worked in the City of London – I had people who did that for me or a calculator, abacus or even slide ruler – had to use shear brain power on this occasion couldn't just delegate the task to a junior. I did make it to zero with just a couple of tuts – not sure if the medical team could do that mental exercise themselves, even with a slide ruler or calculator? No wonder my brain hurt after that exercise.

Also there is that strange feeling of losing awareness of my left arm. One night, during my sleep, I moved my left arm across my body and suddenly I woke up wondering what the heavy weight was across me. I did not even not recognise it as my limb at that point!

I would now admit to some pretty dark days, the following picture captures the mood very well and needs no further explanation. What is really needed more than anything else is **courage and determination** and to **keep moving on**. As your journey is far from being over – let the battle commence Negative days and feelings are going to happen, it's how you choose to look at them that makes them an opportunity to learn or be a downer.

Life has highs and lows. Don't be defeated by the negatives, because those are the moments that will bring you to achieve your best. **Be strong, be powerful.**

Figure 13

As mentioned previously, I never saw 'the light at the end of a tunnel' and decided I still had my children's inheritance to spend and I hadn't finished with my husband yet (sorry girls) – so just like my school reports stated back in the day I decided to pull my socks up and get through this **"brick wall"** and get on with it and try harder. – Although looking back I think it was a side effect of one of my medication. I was just a bugger – the patient from hell. – My character definitely comes from my father and what do I get from my mother? The brains of course. I know my kids talk about me growing up during the flower power era but I was never anti-establishment – just not compliant. I was not totally off my head every day. During the dark days I just had to get on with it and try harder.

I had emotional changes after the stroke, it felt like my whole world as I knew it had just crumbled and the battle for life and survival had just started. What I soon learnt was **to value your achievements, no matter how small and celebrate even the smallest and largest of moves forwards.**

I realised that life changing decisions could have to be made; like should I be looking at retiring and/or becoming a lady of leisure –if I didn't have enough going on, **I had a life changing moment in the form of menopause as well to contend with**.

Quite often I just wanted to hide in my pillow fort. If I am needed, please don't rush to come and get me, I will one day reappear and get on with my life.

Figure 14

It took me quite a while to accept the fact I just wanted to hide and hope it would all disappear or it was all a dream and I would wake up and be back in the kitchen as if nothing had happened at all. If it can happen on TV, then why could it not happen to me as well? Plenty of feeling lost and all at sea.

I am a damaged building in the process of being refurbished and re-wired.

– a work in progress.....

Figure 15

Early rehabilitation can help you to be more independent as you relearn the skills you may have lost, learn new skills and find ways to manage any longer-term disabilities that you may have. During one of my sessions I was tasked with going to the local Sainsbury to buy a number of items – this was all part of rehabilitation back into the community and I got all the items on the list but then when it came to paying I couldn't cope with the money side of the exercise. But hang on a second – I never buy my shopping with cash as I always use a credit card and as I didn't have a protection officer or lady's maid with me who needs to carry cash? Who am I, the queen? – I think not! As long as I got my loyalty points that was all that mattered.

The first few month's rehabilitation is probably one of the most important phases of recovery for many stroke survivors. The effects of a stroke may mean that you must change, relearn or redefine/adapt how you live. Stroke rehabilitation attempts to help you return to independent living.

Rehabilitation doesn't reverse the effects of a stroke. Its goals are to build your strength, capability and confidence so you can continue your daily activities despite the effects of your Stroke.

What you do in rehabilitation depends on what you need to become independent. You may work to improve your independence in many areas. For me these included:

- Self-care skills such as feeding, grooming, bathing, toileting and dressing
- Mobility skills such as transferring, walking or self-propelling a wheelchair
- Communication skills in speech and language
- Cognitive skills such as memory or problem solving
- Social skills for interacting with other people

I now view this whole episode as me being refurbished and – like an old building needing some work being done in order to bring it up to scratch - a work in progress and it is just taking time to find all the relevant blueprints for the final pieces of rewiring - it is also not the end of the book of life but the start of a new chapter in my life.

I didn't want to open my eyes and hence acknowledge the state I was in. I didn't want a support group, but to be in silence beneath the covers. – **It is true that life goes on.** The brain is rewiring itself like a satnav re-calculating a route to the original destination, but from a different start point.

What was one of the most frustrating and frightening part of the stroke was having the difficulty in speaking and understanding. Even today many friends and family find it hard to understand my inability to understand everything that is quite normal for a child to comprehend and take in their stride but slowly my cognitive side of the brain is coming back. However, with busy places and lots of conversations around me, I find it all very difficult to compute/comprehend take in. Such places as train stations and shopping centres – it takes courage and confidence to take it all on board – you just have to bite the bullet and go for it.

You soon forget what normal is!

Negative days and feelings are going to happen; it's how you choose to look at them that makes them an opportunity to learn or be a "downer".

Life has highs and lows. Don't be defeated by the negatives, because those are the moments that will bring you to achieve your best. **Be strong, be powerful**, and with the awesome assistance/support from the Stroke Association, you realise that you can really come out the other end.

I have now formally taken the retirement route as I could never become a lady of leisure as I was never high maintenance nor a princess – I am now an expert at pottering. I have taken the route to occupy myself in a desultory but pleasant way. "I'm quite happy just to potter about by myself".

Synonyms: do nothing much, amuse oneself, tinker about/around, fiddle about/around, tootle about/around, do odd jobs

I am very happy with it! – no more getting up at 6.00am to commute an hour or so on a good day to the office. No more having to contend with tube strikes.

The 'Hospital Game'

 A Long-Term Inmate – don't pass go – don't go to jail - you certainly don't get any money – escape is 'Vorbodden', but the urge is still there!

Figure 16

This is what happened to the last patient who tried to escape - not a happy landing. Luckily there is an A&E department on site, so it is just a short dash to be patched up and back on the ward ready for the next attempt. Perhaps they should try the tunnels next time, but they had better make sure that their cognitive state is sound as there is a whole maze of tunnels under the hospital.

Figure 17

Or maybe just try walking out through the ward doors before lights out – hmm worth a try but wonder how far I will get before anyone notices I am missing?

Figure 18

Hospital gowns are not the most glam nor fashionable – get into your own clothes as quickly as possible, especially those that I ironed one-handed – oh just so slightly creased - with the creases not quite in the right place though! Hospital gowns are worn by patients and are designed so that hospital staff can easily access the part of the patient's body being treated. The hospital gown is made of fabric that can withstand repeated laundering in hot water, usually cotton, and is fastened at the back with twin tape ties. **Arse gap fashion**.........there goes any dignity I had, at least I kept my bum hidden – which actually is an art and not a science – especially when waddling by other people.

Figure 19

Some hospital gowns are floral instead of being plain and if you actually want to be quite trendy then try wearing one slightly off the shoulder it does look rather chic looking or try wearing it with straps in the front and not with straps in the back – at least then your bum won't be hanging out and giving others a good laugh as you waddle by. *The NHS does not run a fashion department.*

Figure 20

•Hot tip for women – a front fastening bra is a must or none at all – your choice- might as well be liberated and let it all hang loose down to the floor if necessary - might not be a pretty sight though, but do give consideration to other patients who might not be able to cope with the sight of it all

Figure 21

Keep a sense of humour!

For a few days my husband couldn't come and visit me and I had to explain where he was –he was working in Iceland – the country, not the shop!

Even now I say – I am not "ga-ga" but I do have a brain injury, especially as I do get some simple things wrong still or forget what day of the week it is. And get very upset and frustrated with myself as I can't remember how to do some very basic every day jobs/functions like how to tie shoe laces or the ingredients for a crumble, even though my occupational therapist spent many an afternoon with me showing me how to tie laces on the same learning toy as I used for teaching my kids how to do it.

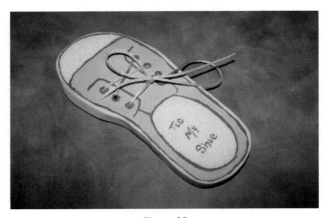

Figure 22

Let me just state that people are always quick to complain and criticise the NHS but I only have the greatest of respect and gratitude to all the nurses and doctors and therapists and health care assistants who treated me during my many month's stay in hospital - you folks are all awesome! Being on the unit was a very humbling and sobering experience. Would I change anything – with hindsight yes – I should have been more cooperative with the initial therapy sessions (a team of therapists received an award – for what I am not sure but I would bet it was for nagging and bullying and not therapy – to this day the team are not saying! – but that's me today – I am still not 100%- still a work in progress but getting there.

My heartfelt thanks to all the teams who helped me through these unchartered waters for me and the family and for putting up with all my antics and weird sense of humour. I do love a bit of sport each day at others expense, you are all such wonderful dedicated professionals/chums.

My First Few Months

Still in Hospital.

The team not only consisted of doctors and nurses but also physiotherapist, which I now know is a very important part of your rehabilitation and recovery. The main focus was getting my posture and balance correct – mind you as a kid I was always being told to stand up straight and to sit properly and take my arms and elbows off the table and they nagged and bullied me into walking again – I hated the exercises and manipulation, massage, skills training and electrical treatment. Try to look at the funny side of things. I was once taken out-side to the car park to be shown how to get into and out of a parked car and the therapist slipped on some stairs at the back of the hospital and hit me in the face – ha! - I am not going to let her forget that one in a hurry. I "dined out" with my black-eye on that episode for quite a few days.

As I have said, humour is so important. I once changed beds *and* rooms and did not tell anyone. Another time I came up with adherence to some obscure religion and claimed it was a religious day of rest or religious festival and couldn't attend the session (none of these religions meant I could walk on water though). The new Jedi religion filled in for the rest of the week. As there really was no therapy on the weekend anyway you might conclude that at that time I was not one of the sharpest tools in the box.

Let's not mention the speech and language therapists you are likely to have some difficulty with swallowing or communicating (- sessions or the clinical psychologists who – can help you deal with emotional problems (plenty of those days especially if a goal was reached) after a stroke which can include anxiety, depression and mood swings sessions – I didn't really play nicely with them but it was good fun at the time – my way of getting some sport in a boring environment (hospital room) let's not mention the dietician – who will recommend a healthy and nutritious diet and if you have swallowing problems, or you could be fed using a tube, or have lost your appetite. according to the kids my ability to swear has improved tremendously – I even now know what some of the naughty words mean!

To me it was like being at boot camp or boarding school (with weekly timetables and uniforms) – except without mid-night feasts again my sense of humour would come out during the sessions and during the course of the day depending on how bored I was at the time. Before I could walk again I was in a wheel chair which was upgraded to an electric one but it was soon taken off me as I was caught doing wheelies down the corridor.

Keep Your Sense of Humour
Not quite as simple a task as you might think. I caused quite a laugh amongst the staff trying to be on time for each therapy session – as I used to work in the city of London and I was known as 'The Late Mrs. Shamah' - not because I was dead, but I was always late for appointments. (In a male dominated environment it was the only decent way I could think of to get noticed and remembered).

Keeping busy

I would sit in the corridor – making the place look busy – loitering with intent and not waiting for a bus. Three buses do not come along together and never the number bus you want anyway!

The last week of my stay on the ward was a hot one! Even with windows open – it was still hot and sticky and the nurses' station had the one and only electric fan on the ward and I was nominated to plan and organise a fan raid – commando style but then I got discharged – so it never happened. Certainly have to embrace the [therapy program in order to get the most out of it. Word of advice always try and be ill in the winter and not in the summer.

One year on:

Oh happy days - As another year comes to an end here's to a year full of health and no more visits or stays however long or short in hospital – I shall keep taking the medication as prescribed (preventative medication) and exercising to keep my fitness and stamina up as well.

Something that they never tell you about is post-stroke seizures. They are really similar to a 'brain itch', not too dangerous, neurologically speaking, but can be really scary.

I had 4 seizures on that first (and only) day starting at the check-out till in a local supermarket. Someone was watching, and did think correctly that I was having either a seizure or a fit and so called an ambulance. I could not speak, but felt like I was dancing, but with less movement than a Zimmer-frame, even though I know that I have my own unique dancing style.

Luckily now with regular medication they are under control. On this occasion even the staff in A&E knew me and I went onto the same ward as before as a precaution and for monitoring – it was like coming home a bit like ground- hog day really been here before – even the food menu had the same choices on it – happy to see nothing had changed – very comforting.

Even my son when he came to see me, went to get his favourite sandwich –hello! Mother is in a hospital bed, ok sat up giggling - boy oh boy Valium is a great recreational drug, never mind your stomach a bit of tender loving care would of not gone a miss at the time and when I was discharged yet again my husband asked for his loyalty card to be stamped, even the car park attendant greeted him like a long lost brother.

My speech has slowed down a lot and softened, but I can now swear like a trooper-according to my children. The kids claim that I don't yell any more at them when I raise my voice – in fact I never 'yelled' at them in fact it was what I call 'motivational speaking for the selective hearing'. My brain doesn't work as fast as it did, especially when I am tired my speech can get rather slurred, when I do try to have a conversation with people who don't know that I was ill, they look at me as if to say do hurry up and get to the point!

Figure 23

One-year anniversary - good times and bad times – I've seen them all and I am still here – happy anniversary to me – bring it on! –still a work in progress though. YOU ARE NOT A VICTIM - live life to the full.

Figure 24

18 months on

Yeah however I still can't accept the fatigue aspect of post-stroke (yawn, yawn, and yawn). I don't want this to sound corny but I am in a much better place today than I obviously was a year or so ago. – All I wanted to do then was to stay in my nest in the hospital bed and not come out – don't know why but that was how it was then. – It felt safe I am building up the confidence to go out and go places and do things/ for myself, although there are still a number of challenges I have to overcome myself. And accept, for instance I still wonder over to the left – almost caused an emergency recently as I was walking along a train platform and I walked over to my left very close to the platform edge thank goodness my husband was with me and pulled me back to the middle of the platform. Also now when I put food on the plate I totally miss out the left side of the plate and get accused of giving more food to one than another at the table – strategy – turn the plate round during dishing up time.

Two years on

Almost 2 years on and I made it to Paris on the train from London all by myself – I did ask for assistance from Eurostar – very helpful and although the French could not understand cognitive impairment – "mais non", but they do understand brain damaged – "mais oui!". My husband was most relieved when I met up with him. I just had to try it by myself.

Tomorrow the world but you can't get round the world via train just yet, but give it time and perhaps one day?

I have just had my two-year check-up and my stroke doctor said to me once I had finished telling him all about my aches and pains in the head. He just sat there and replied "With the size of your stroke which was apparently massive (well the second one was – the bleed the first one was a clot, so I am told and I was not expected to survive the stroke, but survive I did) – stop complaining and just **get on** with it girl, keep soldiering on!" – hmm- perfect bedside manner – no wonder I was the patient from hell- just a right royal bugger. With hindsight I should have been more compliant. Not all patients were able to rebel.

I was, and still am, a handful, strong-willed and terribly independent. I do make mistakes - occasionally.

A couple of interesting things recently happened out of the blue:

I finally managed to swim without flipping over to my left. I guess my core body control has improved.

Another strange thing, one of the functions that I lost was the ability to tell the time from a watch-dial or clock, and this suddenly returned later (like a switch being turned on). Obviously some neuro-pathway opened by itself.

I sometimes smile
and act like
nothing is wrong.
It's called dealing
with shit and
staying strong.

Figure 25

Me today

The positives:

- I live an independent existence, washing, dressing, cooking cleaning, using the bus, walking; volunteering at Stroke Association events.

The negatives:

- Impairments, I can't iron or strip and remake a bed, can't fold clothes and put them away neatly. – not exactly the end of the world

And if you see me on one of my walks please don't think "Ah bless! There goes the crazy woman talking to herself again". I am just telling my left leg to pick up – as it does not always do as it should. My little reminder to my leg does not go amiss. Also if I am slapping myself on the back, please don't think I have swallowed something and it has got stuck I am just congratulating myself for a walk well done.

This 'tragic' event turned our lives upside down.

Through it all, my husband, has been my guiding light. He is the most positive person on earth! He bestowed, positivity, humour, and love all through our journey together. I could not have come out the other side without him. Everything is perfect when I am with him (Ah, ah bless –please pass the sick bucket) - the boy has done great!

Except that once he thought he had found my sports bra when in fact it turned out to be my grandson's vest – not sure why it was in my nicker draw, but (I don't think he found my secret stash of cash!) hey-how. Even without a few frantic mobile phone calls e.g. what cycle to put the washing machine on etc.

Ok, Alright, already, you can stop the mollycoddling, nagging, fussing and leave me to get on with an independent life, and please stop tracking me on my mobile phone.

I know I was a strong person before my strokes, but every now and then I just needed someone taking my hand, offering reassuring words, giving me a hug, and to be there for me.

Figure 26

I am so lucky to have an amazing and loving family and a wonderful circle of friends who kept me going and bought me plenty of food and chocolate which I was not supposed to have – even though it sometimes felt like I was an animal in a zoo and visitors were coming in to look at me. To be honest it felt like I was expected to perform like some sort of freak show but my **heartfelt thanks to you all.** Even though sometimes I felt like charging an entrance fee, had I wanted an audience.

Figure 27

Getting better can take time and does take time, so stay focused and be patient **YOU can do this.** – If I have done it anyone can do it.

Figure 28

You have to keep going and you will get there sooner or later.

As Consistency is the key to success.

Success is never final,

Failure is never fatal,

Its courage that counts

And reach your goal, keep going

(John Wooden)

Believe YOU can **do this** – be determined. **And you're half way there** although you will have to continue to work your 'ass-off' to achieve some results. **Keep up the good work** and strive to come out the other end. Do as a clock does- keep moving forward and keep going, as progress does take time, especially with retraining the brain as it must be retrained slowly, so as not to retrain old bad habits – if only I could remember what those bad habits were? - maybe it is a good job I don't remember them! Rejoice in your victories no matter how small. What is needed more than anything else is courage and determination .and to keep moving on. As your journey is far from being over – let the battle commence. We should always have space for dreams, as they are what keeps us going and gives sense to our lives. So let go of all your worries as a head full of fears will have no space for dreams.

Figure 29

Figure 30

Recollections

Husband's

I wanted to write an account of what happened from my view so that readers might know what to expect as a close observer rather than the stroke victim.

Shani and I were about to celebrate over 30 years of marriage when she had her stroke. We have just celebrated our 34th anniversary and our marriage is stronger than ever.

I often think of our life together as that of a railway journey to some destination city. The stroke has not changed that journey. All it has done is meant that while we are still arriving at that same city, we might be arriving at a different station.

It is strange how the most mundane days can turn into a life changing pivotal moment where all of your preconceived ideas of stability and future suddenly change with no warning.

I was sitting in my downstairs home-office on that Easter Friday afternoon catching up with work and replying to those ubiquitous emails. My son, Michael, was on vacation from his university abroad and he was with his mother in the kitchen.

I heard Shani run down the stairs to our bedroom. She seemed in a rush and I went into the bedroom to see what was up. She was lying on the bed face down. Michael also rushed downstairs saying that he thought that his mum was not well.

I turned her over and tried to speak with her. It was hard to understand what she said. I saw her left side of her face slip away just like the TV adverts I had just recently watched the previous evening. I told her I was calling an ambulance, but she did not want me to. I ignored her.

It is all about your tone and confidence in your message. I called 999/911 and made it very clear that my wife was in the middle of a stroke and that she was exhibiting all the symptoms. – and I needed them now!

I sent my son to get my sister who lives a few doors away, and tried to keep speaking to Shani.

It is strange but you just switch to 'automatic mode'. You know what you have to do, and you really do not have time to think, and as luck would have it within only a few minutes a paramedic arrived.

It was all of a rush. He made a brief examination of Shani and called for an ambulance, telling them to also prepare the hospital for an incoming stroke victim. There was a local Acute Stroke Unit apparently.

Within an incredibly short time the ambulance arrived and Shani was wheeled into the back. I sat with her as I went through some details that I cannot remember with the crewmember and he explained to me that we would arrive in less than 12 minutes! That would be less than 40 minutes since the attack, and I seem to remember that one hour was some magic deadline to have really effective action.

I was still on automatic.

The hospital Accident & Emergency department seemed slow to register and check Shani, but I now know that it was just a matter of a few minutes. She was immediately wheeled away to be scanned. I just paced up and down outside waiting for her to come out. Pacing can be very therapeutic.

I was coming out of automatic mode and with my only personal knowledge about stroke victim being that of seeing the poor shell of a lady being wheeled about in a wheelchair, I was beginning to fear the worst, but it did not occur to me that a stroke could actually be fatal.

Then back to automatic mode.

Shani was wheeled to an empty ward next door to the scanner room and a doctor came and explained that she did in fact have a stroke and that they would need to use a 'clot-busting drug' to remove the clot. He also said that this was not without risk. Having used blood-thinners myself for many years, I understood the risks of getting the clot dissolved without making it easy to bleed internally.

There did not appear to be any choice, and Shani indicated to me that she agreed. – No hesitation as usual.

The drug was given and Shani drifted to unconsciousness.

Up to an emergency ward. She was hooked up to lots of monitors. There was lots of moaning and crying in the ward. It sounded like one of those images from a war-time field hospital on TV – but without the blood.

The doctor explained that there was a good chance that she would recover and she would be asleep until the morning.

I do not remember anything until the next morning. But Shani looked a lot better and seemed to be recovering somewhat. They even had her out of the bed. Panic over! The next few days I stayed with Shani, sleeping in a chair by the bed – the staff were great – and the battery of tests and measurements were taken. Shani started to recover well and even took some steps, walking and talking albeit rather laboured. The doctors started discussing that Shani might be discharged home within a week or even less. She was moved to a general recovery ward where she rapidly improved, walking and talking with greater ease. Even going to the bathroom was starting to be unaided.

So much was the improvement, with a discharge date tentatively planned for the following Friday, that I decided to attend a day meeting in Frankfurt on the Wednesday – just 5 days after the stroke, and 2 days before the planned discharge. Shani was happy with me returning to work and we actually thought that this was no more than a 'blip' or warning for her, such was her recovery. She was very nearly back to normal with good speech and just a very minor limp. She was so well, that we sent our son back to university.

So my normality returned too and I arrived at the flight departure gate at 06:30 ready for the flight. I was walking down the bridge to the aircraft door when I suddenly became overpowered with a wish to see Shani. I thought "Do I really need to go today?"; "Surely I would prefer to be with Shani?"

So I turned around and went back to the gate. I explained about Shani at the hospital and very kindly they arranged an escort back to the carpark, through passport and arrivals.

I did not drive fast but was really feeling relief that I had decided to see Shani. I arrived at the hospital at a little before 09:00 and headed for her room. I saw the nurses on the ward and they told me that she had a good night and they had literally just left her after taking the normal measurements.

I knocked and entered her room. I saw her in mid collapse in the bathroom. As she slid to the floor she appeared to be totally unconscious. My scream to the nurses and lots of rushing about. Machines, monitors, doctors and more specialists.

Then came the worst four weeks of my and Shani's lives........Shani had a bleed in her brain.

I think that I must have been in an almost blind panic after the shock. I do not remember much until I spoke with the head of the Acute Stroke Unit. He did not look happy and as I am good at reading faces, I was beginning to fear the worst. The scans were unable to show up any point of bleed, because Shani's brain was almost completely flooded with blood.

I do not remember who was with me at the time, probably my sister and one or more of the kids. They were with us most of the time during the next few days but honestly it was all peripheral to my perception.

The view was to wait and see if the blood in the brain would dissipate. So we waited.

Shani's best friend, a doctor herself, suggested that the brain should be drained to relieve the pressure. However, with consultation we decided to wait another few days and see if it occurred naturally. Any surgery always carries a risk of bleeding, so we decided to wait and see. I shall never ever forget the look on her friend's face when she first arrived at Shani's bedside. It was the look of expectant catastrophe.

Meanwhile Shani was pretty much out of it. She was connected to feeding tubes, oxygen, and all manner of noisy monitors. Her blood pressure was taken every 15 minutes and her heart rate and oxygenation continually monitored.

This went on for about a week. Shani did not communicate. These were the dark days. I slept at the end of the bed on a mattress. I listened for every bleep of the monitors and woke to look at every blood pressure reading.

I kept family and friends up to date via hourly face-book postings.

I thought that she was lost to us. I consulted our Rabbi as to options in the worst case scenarios. I am very much a believer in being prepared. We discussed issues such as organ donation, keeping the two older of my children in the loop.

Then she started to fight.

A little stronger each day, but stubbornly not eating nor drinking. All she would do was to suck on a swab that was dipped into 'Diet Coke'. Despite the drips and liquid food introduced through a nasal tube, this lack of food was beginning to hurt her, as food is medicine in itself.

She began talking and getting a little bossy. The room was too hot or too cold. It was too noisy. When she started opening her eyes, the light was too bright. The headaches were unbearable.

This went on for another week and every day she got a little clearer and brighter. She found it hard to speak with a tube in her nose and throat. She also was suffering terrible back pains and needed wedges and pillows to get her into a position that was not too painful. They began to angle the bed so she could sit up a little.

Shani being who she is was adamant that she did not want any real food – it was too much like hard work and very tiring.

Shani was never left alone. A rota was set up by friends and family so that there was always someone with her and that gave me a little time to rebuild some order at home and catch up a little on work deadlines, which I did by working from the ward day room and coffee shop. Our friends and family were amazing. My sister was a strong support and the kids were resilient throughout.

Slowly she improved. Shani began to complain about the throat tube, and a compromise was reached that as long as she ate some food they would remove the feeding tube. Then began a period of trying to coax her with cereals, chocolate, energy bars and anything that she would eat. All washed down with 'Diet Coke'.

She started to improve.

The tests and assessments started and Shani started exerting her normal self. She still had lots of trouble processing information and her left arm, hand and leg were not responding. But slowly and surely, every day she began to get better. It was just a blur with all the help that she was receiving.

She began to take a few steps by herself and occasionally I would even take her to the coffee shop to buy her a toasted cheese sandwich. (One of the bribes to make her eat)

After about a month and a half, Shani was ready to be moved to a rehabilitation ward. She was assessed by the ward, which was a unique unit in the NHS system which practiced intense therapy for three or four months rather than the normal drip-feed of therapy. We were very lucky that she was in the same hospital.

The day came for the move to the rehabilitation ward and for the first time since the bleed, I saw light at the end of the tunnel.

Two years after the stroke, I feel privileged to be married to Shani. No one else could have fought back so hard and began to rebuild her life, as someone helping other stroke survivors who were not so fortunate, and actively being involved in volunteering.

I feel that our relationship has strengthened over the past two years, and while there are many ups and downs that we have been through, and no doubt are to come as well, it has been a journey with Shani that I feel blessed to have been part of.

Best Friend's

Shani and I had met at a local working mother's group. In the early days we shared our initial challenges of bringing up a young family with the help of various nannies, au pairs and husbands of course, Shani – as a high powered city worker faced many more sleepless nights, with her twins and 2 other children. Shani would be at her desk in the City of London by 7am whilst my surgery allowed me to start my day a little later- closer to home and enjoying the advantages of a school nearby for my 2 children.

We played tennis together – Shani with her wooden racket and gut strings had won international competitions before she was 18. These early details allow me to describe what the effect of Shani's stroke had in the early weeks. Shani was a lady in full control of a complex work family axis and what happened certainly presented a shattering experience before she fortunately regained her control again – both physically and emotionally. Over the ensuing 30 years as the children grew up and had children of their own – Shani's existence can only be described as that of self-sacrifice – both in terms of her career and personal time. She always put her family first – She has written several books on finance and contributions to financial handbooks. Just before her stroke she was about to start a new post which she was so excited about. I shall never forget the evening when her husband Jon called me. I was having a meal with my family and on hearing the news starting crying in disbelief. How could this happen to someone my age? Even as a GP my thought processes followed the natural stages of hearing bad news. What had caused it – her HRT or her rheumatoid arthritis? – The government had just started a new quality marker to work out stroke risk in patients with rheumatoid arthritis, albeit hers had always been mild. What a relief to see that the damage caused was not too bad as the clot buster drug had been used within 50 minutes. The stroke was right sided so that her speech was affected. Intensive physiotherapy and speech therapy started and Shani was on her way to a recovery. Some brought in food which she relished brought smiles to everyone's faces.

However, a week later Shani's headache got worse – she became drowsier and her left hand lost more strength. She had unfortunately been in the 10% of people who bleed secondary to the clot buster. She lost her confidence, was in severe pain from her head and had leg cramps. She lay in her bed - helpless and powerless. Her family looked on with fear and concern. I felt helpless as my usual approach as a control freak was to speak to lots of my colleagues to see what might be best – e.g. a neurosurgical drainage of the blood. In retrospect this was wrong. I sat at her bedside – rubbed her legs to help her pain – put cold flannels on her brow and tried to control my upset in front of her and the family.

Hugs of support was the most I could do.

Figure 31

I recall that Shani often lay on her bed with her eyes shut during this time – I knew that she was not asleep but felt too distressed to open them. I tried to just keep telling her that she would regain her control with time as indeed she did.

As the following weeks passed – Shani began to improve - at first the smallest of things changed. Her conscious level improved – she was often not asleep and started to engage again with the outside world. In true Shani style she would ask me how I was and about the problems I was having. I was glad to regain the semblance of our mutually supportive relationship. Shani and her mum who I know too, are very much "no nonsense" individuals. I tried to use this approach to reflect back to her in her obviously black moments. I knew that a sense of regaining her self-esteem was vital to her recovery. Her other friends started a food and visiting rota which worked well albeit Shani's mood at this time was variable, not surprisingly.

Her humour was to return when I was reprimanded for leaving a packet of chocolate buttons with her without opening them. Shani would not dream of asking a nurse to help her. This side of Shani's selfless and proud character would serve to block some avenues of therapy to follow but gradually she became more amenable to people's help. The months in the rehabilitation ward were rewarded. When she invited her physiotherapist and I to accompany her to a Michael Buble concert. We went up in a taxi and had the most amazing time. What an emotional feeling to see my friend enjoying herself again.

This journey would not have been possible without the most constant caring support of Shani's wonderful husband – Her amazing sister-in-law was always there too. Her children and grandchildren were always at her side and this allowed Shani to see what she had to fight for.

Family support is often as important as therapists and drugs when something like this happens.

Shani got back home after 6 months' therapy and now leads an independent life when her husband is at work. Typically, she has immersed herself into helping other stroke victims. I'm sure she will continue to progress day- by-day. Her resilience and determination to beat the effects of these two strokes will serve to improve her situation further. We will continue our 3 mile walks I'm sure that I conk out before she does.

Good (and Bad) Stuff to Know

The Stroke Risk

The Stroke risk increases with age as our arteries become harder and narrower. However certain medical conditions and lifestyle factors can speed up the process and increase the risk of having a stroke. Medical problems like high blood pressure, high cholesterol, atrial fibrillation (an irregular heartbeat) and diabetes can increase the risk of having a stroke. Additionally, lifestyle factors, such as diet, drinking alcohol, taking drugs and how active you are can also affect the risk. Just like on the recently aired TV adverts – all rather shocking but none the-less true to form it is just like a fire in the brain and I would advise that if you go out in the sun or sun bathe at any time after a stroke make sure you wear a

Figure 32

sun hat because you don't want your brain to get any more frazzled than it might be already. A stroke is a serious medical emergency that needs urgent treatment as prompt action can help prevent further damage to the brain and delay can result in death or long-term disabilities, such as paralysis.

There are other risk factors which are well within our own control, e.g.

Smoking – the more you smoke the greater the risk Smoking can cause higher blood pressure, which makes the blood stickier and thus increases the chance of a clot developing;

Drinking – too much alcohol, especially binge drinking again can raise blood pressure to a dangerously high level which may cause a blood vessel in the brain to burst;

Similarly, recreational drugs, like ecstasy, increase the risk of a stroke;

Obesity – unhealthy eating and being overweight will not help;

Inactivity – adjust with even just 30 minutes of even gentle exercise 5 times a week. This can lower your blood pressure and keep the heart and blood vessels healthy;

High fat and salt intake - Healthy eating and reducing your intake really can help.

So, how do you help prevent a stroke?
- not guaranteed to work but worth a try

Not an easy question to answer, but making simple changes to your lifestyle could help prevent a stroke. However, you can't change everything, for example your age, but you could stop drinking and smoking and look at eating more healthily and look at reducing excess weight and cholesterol.

But these alone do not guarantee that you do not get a stroke. I always thought I led a healthy life – but obviously I was wrong – maybe I should have drunk and smoked then at least I would have known what to change, but sometimes strokes just happen. I still do not know what onset my stroke. One possibility is that on the day the stroke occurred I miss-balanced on an office chair, over reached and fell off with the arm of the chair giving me a right bang up the back side – it hurt my pride more at the time.

And what about recovery?

How much recovery you will make after a stroke and how long this takes is different for everyone. It all depends, partly on the amount of damage done by the stroke and partly on your general health before the stroke. Recovery tends to be fastest in the first few weeks and months after a stroke, and then slows down, but many people continue to notice changes and improvements over longer periods.

Let me state that every stroke is different and people are affected in different ways as some symptoms can be quite mild and last a short time whilst other strokes may cause more severe and long lasting or permanent damage.

Sometimes you can think you're not improving but **don't be fooled by the slowness of recovery** – It's always there.

Your stay in hospital

Check out the bedside draws/cabinet – bet you find nothing in them – not even a sewing kit - nor a bible nowadays!

A stay on a hospital ward is very regimental – everything runs to a schedule:

- Breakfast 08:00 hrs – tray to be placed on the table over the bed
- Pills 08:15hrs
- Stand by your beds for inspection 08:30 hrs
- Personal hygiene – i.e. use of the bathroom 09:00hrs
- Lunch in the day room at a communal table with "come dine with me on the TV at 12:00hrs
- Afternoon cup of tea 15:15hrs – off the trolley
- Dinner 18:00hrs in the day room again
- Pills 18:00 hrs off the sweet cart
- Bedtime 20:30hrs
- Lights out 21:00 hrs – except the light switch was so high up on the wall it needed one of my roommates to switch the lights off – as the nurses were not tall enough to reach.

Another tip is that if you know you are going to have an eye test on the ward then look at the letters the night before from a distance that you can see them clearly from, then try and remember the order for the test – it can help your brain to function as well – nothing wrong in a little cheating –as a stroke can affect your eye sight as well – it worked every time.

Your stay in a NHS hospital will be different for everyone depending on the circumstances – try to make whatever space you have as homely as possible – with pictures and photos etc. also try and avoid arguments – work any problems out calmly and logically – explain the problem as best you can – it is not worth wasting your time arguing or getting angry – the doctor and nurses are your greatest allies and advocates – when asking questions make sure you understand the answers – if it doesn't sound right to you ask them to explain it again in lay-man terms and in English and not to use medical terms.

You will be cared for on a ward that specialises in your condition. Before you have any treatment the doctor or nurse will explain what is planned and ask if you have any questions or concerns – don't be afraid to ask during the doctors' ward rounds, no matter how silly the question might be, which generally will happen weekly or more frequently if your condition changes at all, or you are to be discharged. Additionally, the specialist teams on the ward are made up of many healthcare professionals, who will help with your care.

The nurses wanted me to make my bed. It takes a good couple of years' study to get the corners right – no fitted sheets in hospital and I wouldn't want to put a nurse out of work and with my cognitive state – there was every chance, and no chance, of me getting it right or even attempting it.

Medicines are an important part of your treatment whilst in hospital and at home – do ask about your medicines –what they are for and how often do you take them and how to take them. Are there any side effects? You should be made aware of and what to do if any occur. When it was medication time I would refer to it as the sweet trolley.

Health Warnings

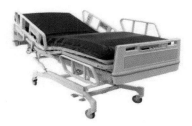

Figure 33

Although things will have changed from what you used to do believe it or not you are still the same person just doing things a little differently and perhaps a little slower than before. But instead don't just watch the clock, but I repeat, do as a clock does - keep moving forward and keep going. Celebrate your successes as many people are frustrated by what they can't do and forget to feel good about what they have started to do again. Always look forward and never backwards.

Some days there were more staff than visitors around my bed – if I wanted an audience I would have charged an entrance fee at the door as they came in. - oh give the girl some peace.

The first question everyone asked was how I was doing and how I was feeling – to be honest how was I supposed to feel? Even now I don't remember what normal is. And quiet please –she is trying to recover from a serious medical condition or hide from the Physiotherapy team – especially if it was a session I didn't want to attend thank you! Tricks of the trade are asking to go to the bathroom or say that due to low blood pressure you have to have a lie down and are feeling quite dizzy- never failed to work, or just had a session and you are exhausted.

Here are some real tips:

Noise and spending your day

- A hospital ward/room can be the most boring place to spend your time;
- But Don't expect to get a rest as there is no rest in a hospital; always being checked and assessed
- If you are unable to get out of bed by yourself, then staff are likely to use a Hoist to get you in and out of bed – it feels like what a beached whale must feel like – so try extra hard!
- Key pointer – no matter what stroke ward you happen to be on be sure not to stand in front of the ward doors at 1 minute to 8am otherwise you could get run over by the wheelchair convoy on their way out for the 'post breakfast cigarette' at the back of the bike sheds. But don't tell sister or matron as they won't be at all amused.
- You will become a clock watcher and a trolley listener. For a fresh jug of water or the sweet trolley (medicine round); or the cart/ trolley to take another set of ops; or the meal trolley – never a good one to wait for- you can't dine out on hospital food. Trolley listening is easy. With the latest government cutbacks obviously WD40 lubricant is definitely now off the procurement list – it is amazing how noisy those trolleys can be.

Privacy

- Privacy and dignity and respect - most hospitals now provide same-sex accommodation whereby sleeping and washing areas are provided for men or women. Only sometimes there might be a single room available on the ward. But in general they are kept for patients who need to be nursed in isolation or barrier nursing.

- Hospital food is really terrible and unimaginative – how many ways can you have Corn Flakes and Rice-Crispies for breakfast? It can seriously damage your health even if you are on a private ward or in a private room it does not mean to you get automatic access/upgrade to the executive menu or order from the al-a-carte menu. Even though food is medicine.....

- Do not seriously try this at home – cereal with orange juice instead of hot or cold milk!

The Bedpan

Figure 34

- Some medication can cause constipation (the staff do like to make sure you are regular) - if you are not they can give you something to make sure you are! (but not prunes).

- Let's not mention bed pans – oh how I do hate them so-why-oh -why? Has no-one invented a soft bed pan it is likely that when a bed assessment/statement has been made you will not be able to go to the bathroom on your own and if the nurses are busy with other patients then a

- Bedpan will be the order of the day? Or even a nappy but be warned – make sure the nurse does not tilt your bed at one end otherwise you will get a wetting!!
- Keep yourself entertained even at the most basic level. For bowel movement, the 'inmates' of the ward once played a mind game with the nurses - we all claimed that we had opened our bowels at the same time that morning! Right at the start of my stay I was having quite a lot of bowel problems and the stuff I was given made me produce a lot of wind – it was a good job there were no naked flames around the place!

Pain control
- If you experience any pain, make sure you let a member of the nursing staff know so they can make sure you are made more comfortable.

What to wear?
- As a consequence of your stroke you might have lost the use of one side of your body and hence washing and dressing could be an issue – when you are able, wear clothes that are easy to put on and take off like track suit bottoms – not the most fashionable but comfy and easy to do up and t-shirts and either comfy big shirts or tops which don't need a lot of doing up. Remember this is not a time for a fashion statement, or cat walk. Socks will become a challenge to put on if you have lost the use of one hand. Sensible shoes without laces or buckles and flip flops for the bathroom and a towelling dressing gown helps to get you dry all over after a shower.
- By the way, get your clothes etc ready the night before. Whenever you get dressed put the bad side in first.

Measuring Stuff

Hospital scales (not weighing or music scales) – there are scales for everything – which are all relative anyway. For example, pain, stools (pictures to help you decide where on the scale your stools are - black and white pictures but soon to be released in techno-colour, exercise effort.

The Pain Scale –A common question but "how painful?" in relation to what? - A paper cut or child birth – please help and give us a clue!

Measuring Pain

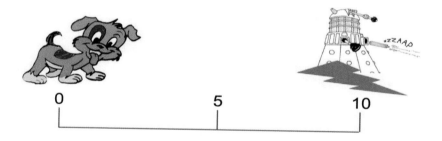

There has to be some way to measure pain so that it can be compared to pain at another time

Figure 35

Measuring Pain using Squirrels;

I came up with my own 0 to 10 scale of pain, equating the number of squirrels cracking nuts inside my head at any one time:

Level	Number of Squirrels	Amount of Pain
10		Extreme pain – I need relief NOW!!! – unbearable – please sedate me!!! (like giving birth)
8		Bad pain – I need painkillers urgently
5		Moderate pain – some painkillers would be nice (like a paper-cut)
3		Light pain – It would be good to have a painkiller soon
1		'Normal' pain – I don't need painkillers really
0	(no squirrels)	I have never got to this stage yet in two years!

For the first two months after my stroke, I was hosting a continuous party with ten squirrels in my head. Then they started to get bored and by the end of the second year, I have a very lonely squirrel looking for something to do!

How long will I need to stay in hospital?

The length of stay required for stroke assessment and rehabilitation varies considerably, and will depend on when the doctor is satisfied with your progress and only then you could be transferred to a stroke rehabilitation unit. Rehabilitation means different things to different people. To me it was like being sent to boot camp (a.k.a. boarding school) with colour-coded staff uniforms and session timetables. It makes it all sound as if I was an alcoholic or 'drug addict'. At the same time, it provides an ideal therapeutic environment for the retraining in all daily living activities.

Avoid becoming institutionalised

Do not become institutionalised

Figure 36

Therapy, Physiotherapy & Rehabilitation

A very important key to getting moving again is therapy, and the more therapy that you can get as soon as possible. It is a very important concept, and one which I didn't fully take on board right away or understand. As an intelligent person I should have known better. And remember you are not an invalid – get out of bed and get moving and sit in a chair. Very important as there will be many 'down' days.

By the way, the difference between occupational therapy and physiotherapy is that Physiotherapy gets you walking whilst occupational therapy gets you dancing!

Rehabilitation will begin when your doctor determines that you're medically stable and able to benefit from it. Most rehabilitation services require a doctor's order. Under your doctor's direction, rehabilitation specialists provide a treatment program specifically suited and designed to your needs. The number of services you receive will depend on your needs.

Rehabilitation services are provided in many different places:

- Acute care and rehabilitation hospitals
- Long-term care facilities
- At home, through home health agencies
- Outpatient facilities

You may be involved in rehabilitation in some or all of these settings. It depends on your needs and what type of rehabilitation program will be best for you.

Recovering after a stroke can be long-term. It involves getting the proper rehabilitation and also getting to know /educating yourself about what type of stroke you had and what a stroke is, mentally and emotionally coping with the recovery process will not be easy and this takes time – so be prepared.

Figure 37

Some people who have had a stroke will make a good recovery, quite quickly. Unfortunately, not everyone gets better. The aim is for rehabilitation early. All this against the clock, as the original blue-prints are starting to fade! It is like having to re-wire your brain

Rehabilitation

Helps you to cope and adapt to your situation so you can become as independent as possible

Figure 38

to relearn any skills that you may have lost, learn new skills, and find ways to manage any long term disabilities.

Aims of rehabilitation

Rehabilitation means different things to different people. For some it is an active process of change whereby independence and lost abilities can be restored and the patient and family can find ways of successfully adapting to a degree of ongoing disability. For others; perhaps those with profound neurological damage, it may be a case of assessing the true extent of disability and establishing the best way of managing a range of complex problems in the longer term to maintain dignity, comfort and safety.

Overall rehabilitation aims to:

- Restore lost abilities and to compensate for remaining difficulties where possible
- To provide support, information and advice to enable patients and/or their families to make appropriate choices about their future
- To enable patients to find ways to fulfil their potential, even though this potential may be limited by the extent of damage to the brain and various systems.

The Pace of rehabilitation

During the first couple of weeks you will meet all the different disciplines involved in your rehab programme – each one will spend time trying out therapy and rehab approaches. Assessing your difficulties and needs. This helps to identify goals for your stay and potential discharge date. This initial period is often referred to as assessment but rehab is ongoing throughout this period. In the first few weeks your timetable may be a little quieter but this will change as you become abler to take part in more therapy sessions and group work. Although they will normally be activities every day you may not have sessions with each therapist every day. Also as discharge day nears the number of sessions will decrease as the majority of time will be spent doing assessments again and comparing your progress against what it was today compared to when you arrived. Upper limb rehab it never occurred to me to remind the physiotherapist that thankfully I am right handed and what they were asking me to try and do things with my left hand (which I have lost the use of) I would not have naturally done any way as a right-handed person.

Each timetable is individual to your own rehab needs, it will include one-to-one and joint treatments with qualified staff as well as planned activities to carry out on your own during the week. Based on your needs there could be planned group sessions that you could be invited to attend. For example, discussion group, or music therapy – also good to get you talking again via singing songs like happy birthday or quiz group. – Great way of getting to know fellow inmates as well. There is nothing wrong in asking for some rest time after a session or in between sessions.

Goal setting

You are likely to be asked to identify the overall aims you wish to achieve during your stay but be careful what you say otherwise before you know it – it has become a goal – make sure it is realistic and achievable.

Also **Goals** must be set that are small, manageable, time \ (smart) and Stay motivated as your goal is never out of reach but to be on the safe side Plan for setbacks.

My goals were:

- To attend a Michael Buble concert at the O2 centre. – such a tonic but I did go with a doctor and a member of the Physiotherapy team – what is the point of having a child in the music industry – if you can't ask for a favour! Nice to clap your hands! [DONE!]

Figure 39

- Manipulate my hand and fingers to make a really rude gesture (pretty hard to do!), This simple movement involves a number of key movement for the arm, hand, wrist and fingers all at the same time [DONE!]

- To see my son's graduation abroad. This occurred the following week after my discharge. Boy was that a tough trip! [DONE!]

Remember to keep going and be courageous reach your goal – Stay motivated, your goal is never out of reach.

"You may wish to reasses your global domination goals: perhaps talk to your line manager about alternatives to extermination"

Figure 40

The Team

Each patient will have a named nurse who has responsibility for co-ordinating your care, supported by a health care assistant. My nurses are either the red or blue teams. – Hence my mention of uniforms.

Keyworker – likely to be from one of the professions in the therapy team. This person will be your link person who will co-ordinate your rehabilitation on the unit- **she who must be obeyed** (again no names will be mentioned)! One of my ward roommates would stand outside the door and watch out for her and give me the nod when she saw her coming.

Key working sessions – your named/senior nurse will attend some of your key working sessions to review your care and to address any concerns you may have during your stay. Other members of the multi-disciplinary team may join the sessions as well depending on the issues raised

Multi- disciplinary teams – occupational therapists; - will help you find new ways of doing things like getting washed and dressed as well as giving advice on equipment before leaving hospital as basket weaving it most certainly is not nor painting by numbers.

Physiotherapists; physiotherapy is an important part of rehabilitation helping you to regain as much mobility, muscle control and strength as possible and build up muscle strength again.

Physiotherapy

Physiotherapy helps restore movement and function when someone is affected by injury, illness or disability. It takes a holistic approach that involves the patient directly in their own care. They treat people of all ages, helping them manage pain and using a

"Well, this certainly buggers our plan to conquer the Universe."

Figure 41

number of methods to aid recovery. Although they're often thought of as just dealing with musculoskeletal problems, physiotherapists are trained healthcare professionals who work in many areas. When a stroke causes damage to the part of the brain that controls movement, physiotherapy is an important part of rehabilitation, helping you to regain as much mobility, muscle control and strength as possible.

Top tip; if you have the first session of the day, so as not to be late, maybe you should consider to go to bed the night before ready dressed.

Electrical Stimulation – Electricity can be fun!

A tool that they might try to stimulate your muscles with is Electrical Muscle Stimulation (EMS), also known as NeuroMuscular Electrical Stimulation (NMES) or Electromyostimulation. This is the elicitation of muscle contraction using electric impulses.

EMS has received increasing attention in the last few years, because it has the potential to serve as:

- a tool for healthy rehabilitation and preventive tool for partially or totally immobilized patients;
- a testing tool for evaluating the neural and/or muscular function in vivo;
- a post-exercise recovery tool.

The impulses are generated by a device and delivered through electrodes on the skin in direct proximity to the muscles to be stimulated. The impulses mimic the electrical potential coming from the central nervous system, causing the muscles to contract. The electrodes are generally pads that adhere to the skin. I had this device on numerous occasions and my husband has a worst sense of humour than me and thought it would be a laugh to set it to its highest setting. Boy oh boy, did I nearly hit the ceiling!

Occupational therapy

This provides practical support to enable people to facilitate recovery and overcome any barriers that prevent them from doing the activities (occupations) that matter to them. This helps to increase people's independence and satisfaction in all aspects of life. "Occupation" refers to practical and purposeful activities that allow people to live independently and have a sense of identity. This could be essential day-to-day tasks such as self-care, work or

Figure 42

leisure. Basket weaving it most certainly is not. The difference between occupational therapy and Physiotherapy is that Physiotherapy gets you walking whilst occupational therapy gets you dancing – well that one didn't work out too well!

Clinical Psychologist

The Clinical Psychologist helps you to manage your emotions and mental processes including anxiety, depression and mood swings. They can also help if you have problems concentrating, planning or remembering things.

"Every time you use that word you exterminate part of yourself."

Figure 43

A psychologist actually had to confirm that I was not suicidal but I was in fact sane, otherwise I could not be let near an open window. Some had a train of thought that actually questioned this assessment and a copy of the psychologist's qualifications were asked for just to check that her assessments were being analysed correctly- they had never come across anyone with a northern sense of humour before- so, it was ok to have the windows open fully during sessions as I was not about to dive through them or jump out.

Speech and Language Therapy

A stroke can affect your ability to communicate. Speech and language therapists can suggest ways to help you communicate using exercises, speech, reading and writing, and also explain to family and friends how they can help you communicate. Sometimes these may be alternatives such as writing, drawing and gestures.

Figure 44

Music Therapy

We all respond to music. Some in other ways than others. But do not dismiss its power to help. Remember that you do not need experience with musical instruments

Figure 45

Visiting home from hospital

It is good to get home. The first time at home can be a little worrying as you may find you are unable to do some of the things you were doing previously. Visiting home for a day or overnight can be an exciting time for you and your family. As well as enjoying spending time with your family, it is a great opportunity to try out in a real-life setting some of the things you have been doing with therapists and nurses in the stroke unit – this will give you and the team vital information about your abilities be warned most of the time at home is likely to be spent shopping and paying bills and generally catching up with general every day activities. And trying to get some normality back into your life. Trying to take control back.

Assessment of the home the occupational therapists may arrange for the necessary equipment if required.

Building up time at home slowly

Just a day visit / single overnight stay/weekend leave is used as the aim towards a home discharge. Typically – guidelines are written and prepared as these provide recommendations in order to help you to manage safely around indoors and outdoors and conducting activities. Also a health and safety assessment will be needed to be conducted before any home visit to make sure you will be in a safe environment.

More than likely out in the community again you might be referred to as a stroke survivor rather than someone who has had a stroke because you would only be a patient in hospital for a limited time but please note again that not all strokes are the same I have now learnt the hard way that rehabilitation works best when you are in the right frame of mind and works best when you are cooperative and not just in it for the fun/sport and you are working together as a team with the therapists. As they say there is no I in team.

Learn to pace yourself, once you have been discharged as this should help you cope with the subject of possibly being fatigued. And finish one job at a time – don't get distracted.

The Case Conference

The case conference (AKA escape committee) will include all the team involved in your rehabilitation and provides an opportunity/forum to discuss the results of any assessments, the goals you may be hoping to achieve and any plans for leaving hospital. It is also a chance to discuss any other issues of concerns

This meeting usually takes place 3 to 6 weeks into admission at the end of this meeting a potential discharge date will be given but it can be brought forward and likewise can be put back as well.

The meeting, along with rehab sessions slow done towards the end and becomes more a case of assessments and comparing where

Figure 46

you were at the start to where you are at the end.

The Discharge Plan

The aim of the discharge plan is to be sure that your care is continued after leaving hospital. Usually you get a home visit to assess the practical help that you need, like hand-rails, bath stools etc. Continuity is important to ensure that your rehabilitation continues, otherwise there is a chance that any progress you have made may be lost.

Life after a Stroke - Re-Building My Life

Stuff that Can Happen

Fatigue

Fatigue is an overwhelming feeling of tiredness. It can be debilitating enough to stop you from doing everyday things like getting dressed, going to the shops or preparing food, and cannot be put right simply by sitting down and having a cup of tea.

Fatigue is a subjective experience, but it has been described as "hitting a brick wall" or "like no other tiredness I've felt before".

So what causes fatigue?

Fatigue is very common among people with neurological conditions. Sometimes the specific cause of your fatigue may be unclear. It can be part of the healing process.

A sign of healing

When recovering from surgery, or a sudden event like a brain injury or subarachnoid haemorrhage, fatigue is to be expected. That's because your body and brain are working hard to compensate for your injury. They are doing all the things you used to do, but also using extra energy in the healing process. If you were very stressed or overworked before, this will also have an effect on how fatigued you feel during your recovery. As you begin to recover, the fatigue may go away or happen less often, although you may still get tired or fatigued more easily than you used to.

Living with a neurological condition is not easy. You may need to get used to new ways of doing things, such as using public transport instead of driving, or learning to use a wheelchair. Getting used to your new way of life may be very tiring, especially at first. You may experience sleep problems, perhaps due to pain, discomfort or bladder weakness. Depression is often a cause of fatigue. You may, understandably, feel stressed, angry or depressed because of the changes to your life. Some medications, such as anti-epileptic drugs or analgesics, may make you feel very tired and could contribute to an overall feeling of fatigue. Triggers for fatigue physical activity might not tire you out as much as mental effort: but put me in a crowded room for 15 minutes with a lot of conversation and the fatigue would hit me.

Partial loss of vision

Sometimes there may be changes in your vision after a stroke.

While your physical vision may be un-impaired, because of the relative strengths of the left and right part of the brain, you may suffer from Attention Deficit. This is when you do not pay as much attention to one side of your overall vision compared to the other. It is a lot like seeing out of the corner of your eye – except it may encroach more than usual. In my case it was about 20% off my left side vision. Which can make it hard to read or use a computer without retraining yourself to move your head a little. It does get less noticeable in time, but it can be tiring in big crowds or busy locations.

Post Stroke Seizures

One paragraph I didn't expect to write, and what they don't tell you is about **post-stroke seizures.** Some stroke patients can have a seizure, repeated fits (or similar to epileptic) attacks. However only a small percentage will have an episode and it usually happens within the following couple of weeks after a stroke.

So what causes a post-stroke seizure? In effect cells in the brain communicate with one another and with nerves and muscles. A seizure is a sudden abnormal burst of electrical activity in the brain and this can lead to a seizure.

In effect, it is like an itch that needs scratching.

The good news is that they are not too dangerous — apart from physical damage when falling — but they are VERY, VERY, SCARY. It feels like you are dancing. But do not worry. Medication can usually prevent them from recurring, and if you have not had any after 6-9 months, it is unlikely that you will.

A Strategy

While every stroke is different, some type of disability or physical limitation is common. Setting reasonable, step-by-step goals regarding these three important areas of your life may be a good next step for you:

- **Living your life as fully and comfortably as possible**
- **Recovering as much independence and mobility as possible**
- **Staying safe while returning to activity (preventing falls)**

Your attitude and effort matter most of all. Many stroke survivors who follow a rehabilitation plan regain significant function. The more you use your body, the better you will get.

All the Nevers
- **Never stop trying!**
- **Never stop believing!**
- **Never give up!**
- **Never stop practising your skills!**

Attitude is Everything

My attitude changed once I decided to move on and make the most of the bad situation – accept the event. A good one with Physiotherapy – which I still do today is with any exercise you will be told how many times to do it – if I was told 20 and they were not counting I would then be asked how many have I done the answer would always be above the number I was asked to do. I have still not learnt from my mistakes to this day and am quite stubborn – just to show that the stroke has not changed my character.

Learn to be patient, as it can take time to recover what you have lost. It's very hard to keep motivated but you can keep exercising and keep positive. everything that was happening was too much for me to compute and take in-had to adjust to limited brain capacity – everything becomes a blur – in fact I would say I felt lost, but I am getting it back. That is the trick. Do not give in!!

Even though, the best plans can get side-lined unexpectedly - look ahead at your week to anticipate any challenges and always have a 'Plan B'.

Think 'Peter Pan Style'. Let the ground move beneath your feet, sing in the shower, whip up your favourite meal, spend time with a great friend, basically do whatever it takes to bring "magic" to the gloomiest of days.

Having sex after a stroke

There is no medical reason that should restrict your sex-life. However, foreplay such as being chased around the bedroom might have to be curtailed for a while. Remember that swinging from chandeliers may not be advisable as well.

Sexual difficulties can be the result of many factors including psychological, such as low mood, and physical problems, such as weakness or paralysis. Often a little information and reassurance will be enough to overcome these issues

Common factors that may reduce your drive are:

- Anxiety;
- Emotional;
- Less sensitivity
- Fatigue
- A combination of some or all of the above factors

Fatigue after a stroke

Again back to talking about fatigue……

Is this one of the most common effects of a stroke?

It can make you feel unwell and like you are not in control of your recovery. The signs of fatigue are not always obvious to other people and so they may not understand how you are feeling. Learn to pace yourself by taking proper breaks before or after doing things. Even gentle activities like talking or a car journey and eating a meal can be tiring. Learn to listen to your body. If you are exhausted during the day then rest. This could either be sitting or lying down or sleeping. There are no rules about how much time to rest for. However, if you are not sleeping at night then try resting less during the day. Hospital is no place for a rest as always someone taking your vitals or asking you questions.

Don't make it hard for yourself by trying to do all the things you used to do, or at the same speed. It can be helpful to lower your expectations of what you can achieve for a while, so you can build up stamina and strength slowly again. You may feel you are going backwards, so increase your activity gradually. And learn to pace yourself.

What is post- stroke fatigue? – Everyone feels tired sometimes. It is a normal part of life and can happen for all sorts of reasons, such as if you haven't slept well or have had a very busy day. Usually you feel better after resting.

Fatigue after a stroke is different for everyone– you may feel like you lack energy or strength and constantly feel weary or tired. Post-stroke fatigue does not always improve with rest and is not necessarily related to recent activity. So it is not like typical tiredness. You might be inclined or tempted to dismiss how you are feeling or stoically carry on regardless. However, if you do ignore fatigue you could be storing up problems for the future and you are not giving yourself the best opportunity to recover.

So why do I feel so tired?

It is likely to be a mixture of physical and emotional factors that are contributing to you experiencing fatigue after a stroke, even though it is different for everyone. In the early weeks and months after a stroke your body is healing and the rehabilitation process takes up a lot of energy so it is very common to feel tired. Additionally, you are also more likely to have lost strength and fitness whilst being in hospital or as a result of the stroke. Although this does not always mean you will have post-stroke fatigue. In the longer term, having a physical disability also means your energy is being used in different ways. For example, walking and completing other daily tasks/activities may well take up much more energy than they did before the stroke, making you more likely to feel tired. You have to accept that you perhaps can no longer do as many jobs as you used to or tackle at once – don't dwell on it for too long and do try to keep a stiff upper lip – I know it is not easy in some cases to accept this situation – to this day I still can't accept the fact that I **am no longer superwoman** nor a multi-tasker.

Figure 47

I am trying now to work my way through this by having structured exercise a couple of times a week. Stroke survivors often experience frustration and fatigue trying to maintain the same lifestyle they had before their stroke. For many stroke survivors, it's impossible to return to their old activities and schedules, stroke survivors can benefit by implementing new routines and adapting new ways of life. Definitely my **confidence was destroyed** and with my left upper arm weakness and speech problems in addition to the fear and confusion about what happened combined with fatigue it has taken their toll.

I now have to think hard especially when crossing the road – I now always have to cross on the green man when I am out alone whereas before I would perhaps have played chicken with the traffic. Just a lack of confidence more than anything else. I can't judge how fast oncoming traffic is going. The green cross traffic code is now my new best friend.

Before a stroke, most people can link their fatigue to a specific source or object. However, after a stroke occurs, many survivors are unable to identify the source of their fatigue. If stroke survivors are able to understand what is causing their exhaustion, they can adapt new routines and have an overall higher quality of life.

Here are three ways to help you identify and manage your fatigue.

1. Keep a fatigue diary. Keep a record of when fatigue occurs, so you can identify specific objects or actions which may be causing it. Discuss your daily routine with your general care practitioner, physical therapist and members of your rehabilitation team. Your doctors can help identify activities that are causing your fatigue and discuss new ways to approach these activities.

2. Plan Your Activities. After a stroke, it's important to plan your activities. This will help minimize stress and fatigue. Make sure to bring the necessary medication, food and water with you and leave time for rest. Make a list ahead of time of all the things that you need for the day.

3. Adjust Your Diet. Your body processes every food differently. If you have a long day ahead of you, consider eating energy-packed foods to help your body manage fatigue. Some examples of energy packed foods include:

- Dark chocolate
- Pumpkin seeds

- Red bell peppers
- Tea
- Walnuts

Decision Making

It is called Executive Dysfunction.

Difficulties with decision making – is a common problem – it is one element of a broader set of mental skills that have been called' executive functions' these are the skills needed to enable us to deal with problems that arise in everyday life and to cope with new situations. Both minor and some major.

Decision making involves many different cognitive functions working together:

Long-term memory (how have I dealt with similar situations in the past? What choices have I made before?). Working memory; because decision making involves a lot of different processes, this means that if any one of these processes is affected, then decision making may be impaired, however affected people are affected in different ways

However, strategies to cope can be put in place – for example for me the plan of action is simple- write everything down and ask for guidance and then if still uncertain – ask again for the situation to be explained in simple terms.

Make sure you are aware of the problems and understand the work around. Have a plan B, in case plan A does not work out.

Working-out how to improve the ability to make decisions, to be better at solving problems, planning, following through with plans may best be done with the help of a professional in rehabilitation such as an occupational therapist or clinical psychologist. The first step in rehabilitation is understanding the problem, but with something as complex as decision making or problem solving difficulties this may not be straightforward, which is why the help of a professional may be important.

Executive dysfunction is an umbrella term for loss of many abilities including:

- Social behaviour
- Self-awareness
- Decision making
- Planning and organisation;
- Flexible thinking;
- Multi-tasking;
- Solving unusual problems;
- Controlling emotions;
- Motivation;
- Concentrating and taking in information;

It is a term for the range of cognitive, emotional and behavioural difficulties which often occur after brain injury. Impairment of executive functions is common after acquired brain injury and has a profound effect on many aspects of everyday life.

Me today – I am having to learn to pace myself and understand my limitations and learning to finish one task off before moving onto the next one – no more being a multi-tasker. In fact, our brains were not made for multi-tasking, and it is in fact a development of

Figure 48

today's life style. Some would say that I was a control freak and micro manager – I still can't multi-task and have to write things down.

Ongoing Physical Issues

I am still having problems with my left shoulder. With acute pain from the stroke affecting other older issues. Also my left hand is still not 100% functional, so I am doing my Physiotherapy exercises regularly and I do try to involve it in everything. I have even named my hand and left shoulder to try to make them more personal.

They also remind me that they are still with me. I get a continuous pins and needles and sensitivity down my left arm and leg. It makes it hard to have a shower, but apparently a small number of stroke survivors get this quite badly. – I guess that I am lucky.

Strangely, I also can't tell the difference between cold and hot water and I cannot control /regulate my body heat. So no more swimming in outdoor pools!

Retrospective

I hate how this illness has hurt my husband and family. But we will grow old, grey and get wrinkly together.

Figure 49

Disappointments, challenges and failures are not meant to destroy us but, they are meant to strengthen and challenge us. Don't ever give up if you have your mind you can relearn the rest, rejoice in your victories no matter how small or great. When you are no longer able to challenge the /a situation, we become challenged to change ourselves.

'Incredible change happens in your life when you decide to take control of what you do have power over instead of craving control over what you don't'.

Some words that sum up a stroke:

Devastating; Debilitating; Personal; Life-changing; Challenging; Hope; Frustrating.

Some words and phrases that you will love or hate:

- Victim – YOU ARE NOT A VICTIM
- Patient – YOU ARE NOT AN INVALID
- Survivor – YOU ARE A CHAMPION, NOT JUST A SURVIVOR
- Impairment – YOU HAVE CHALLENGES TO OVERCOME, NOT IMPAIRMENTS
- Strategies – REALLY MEANING 'WORK-AROUNDS'
- Learn to live with it – THAT IS EASY FOR SOMEONE ELSE TO SAY
- Use it or lose it – ALWAYS JUST TRY YOUR BEST…AND A LITTLE BIT MORE!
- I am tired of being tired
- It's the new norm.

Some good final (and maybe repeated) pointers:

- There is no point in harking on about the old days and what you could do – if you want to do it still – find a way to do it!

- **Keep your sense of humour and keep positive** – wonderful tonics for recovery **but be resilient**, even though you might feel that you will never smile or laugh again,
- Especially when you are frightened and wondering what the hell was happening to you, even though it can feel that life is very unfair you will come out the other side eventually.
- Questioning 'why me?' will not change or solve anything
- Learn to cope with strategies –complaining won't change the outcome but a positive attitude will. I know that to start with, a good majority of stroke victims start off depressed and have a grieving phase of how life has changed or will change – it is the new normal that will make life so odd at times, not just for the patient but also for the family, there could be an awful lot of adjustments to be made not only in the short -term but long-term as well. You have to learn to adapt one day at a time. There are a lot of changes going on as your brain is remapping.
- Although you will have to continue to work your 'ass-off' to achieve some results. So keep up the good work and strive to come out the other end!
- **Patience and determination** will become part of everyday life. Give yourself credit for how far you have come not just how far you have to go
- Recovering after a stroke can be long term. It can be a long slow frustrating recovery. Sometimes, it can feel as if your old self has died. This illness has taken away my happiness in many things that I loved doing
- It involves getting the proper rehabilitation and educating yourself about the type of stroke that affected you. You need to mentally and emotionally cope with the recovery process which all takes time. But it was like being stuck in quick sand – I was no longer the heart and soul of the family. I had to give it all up for the stroke.

- Do not be in denial – treat what you have lost as a kind of bereavement, and work within the new reality.
- Most importantly of all, you need to believe in yourself. What defines us is how well we rise after falling and the main point is never to give up as great things take time - just look at Rome! In some cases, a very long- time but keep on trucking! And you need to **believe** in yourself and develop a **'can do' attitude**

Figure 50

- Life is like a camera focus on what's important. **Capture the good times; develop from the negatives** and if things don't work out, take another shot. Success is never final; failure is not necessarily fatal. It is courage that counts.
- Life is too short to not be grateful for every moment that we are alive- today I have so much to be thankful for.

Figure 51

- With hindsight I should have been wiser and 'towed' the party line during therapy and treatment.

Remember:

You are still the same person/character inside as you were before a stroke – nothing changes your character etc. you are still very much intact…. I am still the stubborn cow today as I always was. I still have my old sarcasm, wit and humour!

You must have a can do attitude which won't be easy at first but it is a very important state of mind to have – YOU CAN WIN!

Contact Details for Stroke Association UK:
www.stroke.org.uk
Stroke Helpline +44 303 303 3100

Printed in Great Britain
by Amazon.co.uk, Ltd.,
Marston Gate.